LEAVING TROY

poems by

Joshua Kulseth

Finishing Line Press
Georgetown, Kentucky

LEAVING TROY

Copyright © 2025 by Joshua Kulseth
ISBN 979-8-89990-139-3 First Edition
All rights reserved under International and Pan-American Copyright Conventions. No part of this book may be reproduced in any manner whatsoever without written permission from the publisher, except in the case of brief quotations embodied in critical articles and reviews.

Publisher: Leah Huete de Maines
Editor: Christen Kincaid
Cover Art: Claude Lorraine (1644)
Author Photo: Joshua Kulseth
Cover Design: Elizabeth Maines McCleavy

Order online: www.finishinglinepress.com
also available on amazon.com

Author inquiries and mail orders:
Finishing Line Press
PO Box 1626
Georgetown, Kentucky 40324
USA

Contents

Diomedes Fights With The Gods 1
Subject 2
Minotaur 4
Concrete 5
Nisus And Euryalus 6
Gun 8
Teucer 10
Skipping Stones 11
Thrall 12
Ajax 13
Enigma 15
At The Stockyard 16
Inheritance 17
Tracks 18
Quilts 19
Posts 20
Logging 21
The Boy And The Map 22
Grade School Mythology 23
Through The Peephole 24
Dance 25
Ducklings 27
Words Like Ours 28
Picture Of Us 29
Helen 30
Glass 31
Presence 33
Quotidian 34

Feet	36
Jesus's Knees	38
Eucharist	39
Polites	41
Shoes	42
Pockets	43
Hiding Places	44
Agamemnon	45
Dad's Naps	46
Old Man	47
Beating	49
Martha And Tooter	51
Barn	52
Harvest	53
Broody	55
Achilles	56
Hector	57
Charity	58
Reflection	59
Raising The Hunley	60
New Jerusalem	62
Leaving Troy	63
Horses	65

For my mother

DIOMEDES FIGHTS WITH THE GODS

It's not easy, being devout:
the tributes, burning this or that throat-cut animal,

never skimping the best or neglecting
offerings poured on altars and in the sea,

for victory and safe travels.
Of my loot the gods get first fruits,

so I'm content with this cut-rate gear—
good enough anyway in a fight

I could rout a flank with trashcan lid and broom handle.
And for all this I'm only *second*, after Achilles,

who spits on favors and eats the best meats alone
or with the stolen daughters of Apollo.

I wounded Ares, for god's sake, right there
under the gates, and when I was told to refrain I did,

though I'd fully run those Trojan dogs through,
whimpering back to their wives.

I jump when told and know how high
without having to ask.

Honorless, still I honor men and gods better than anyone.
Is it too much to ask

to be named, spoken of
as more than a supporting role on the edge of history?

Don't forget me, who read
what little is left to say of what I've done,

working in heat some great deed,
and after, gone for good.

SUBJECT

A man on the train is preparing for rain, begins
unpacking exactly all he owns,
old clothes, mostly:

jacket first, then another, tying all in a ball
and placing them neatly
in a plastic bag,

moving to the next; something small this time.
He handles it carefully, unfolding,
waterproofing

in whatever ragged plastic he has: a single latex glove,
a bag and shower cap, restoring,
once he's finished, everything

to his bag and bucket. Now he covers himself
with lotion, first head and hair,
then everywhere

until it all dissolves, hands, fingertips, arms
up to his elbow, hiking pants
above the knee—

poor legs: starving, veined, thirsty
for what he gives them, lathered thick and white,
all while

darting angry looks at the women nearby
rolling their eyes,
who rattle

under breath something lost. He leaves
his sleeves rolled and the hem
of his pants. Ignoring all

now, he props his feet on the pole
in defiance, I guess
of the rest—

snorts, starts to nod off, his shoes now making one
long streak down the pole.
The work all done,

I start to write, embarrassed, only daring
now and then
to scribble what I can,

looking up like a painter, my strokes
covering his snoring
figure, asking

the man in my mind to stop squirming, sit up straight;
no, you can't leave yet,
I've got to get it right.

MINOTAUR

It was my father's bull-headed
beastliness blessed me with this form,
with only the gods'

sense of humor and a few trinkets to keep
me busy between murders—and fleeing
would see me shot-through,

crossing the threshold of this great
puzzle they've stuck me in, the solving
only sacrifice for a handful

lucky enough to die.
My fate to fester here
with all the time in the world—

but who'd have me, if one night I stole
with what stealth gods gave a bull
into the unknown, untried life

waiting on the other side?
At least I'm fed and have my bed,
and quiet enough to think.

It's terrible, this loneliness; and sometimes
the fleas get me so raw with scratching.
I wish I had even some other animal,

but it's only ever the killing;
and it gets old, killing.
I'm not the bull I used to be.

My mother used to sing to me
in the room where I nursed,
before I was taken up.

I've been trying lately to remember
the songs my mother would sing,
but can't get it right.

CONCRETE

> *I remember the guys I was with then*
> *and how hard they were to know.*
>   C.K. Williams

On the hundred-degree summer days
we hauled bags of concrete up six flights of stairs
with the buckets, tools, and heavy mixer
made heavier by caked-on concrete
hardening faster than we could scrape it off.

Even the most level headed of us held nothing back,
spraying the place with curses, and each other
with concrete—tools and buckets, bottles thrown
across the room: none of us free
from the choking strain of heat

except the boss, thirty-something, veteran
of Iraq: three years a Marine, three on an aircraft carrier reading
every book in the library. I asked him once
how he kept it together: *when you've seen men*
vaporized by IEDs, nothing else bothers you.

He said it simply, like a child, his simplicity splintering
on me like quartz, light-struck, in the pickup truck
now impossibly fleeced with a million grey specks,
shedding from our shirts, spreading
over every surface. I was afraid

that whatever it was I was, it wasn't enough;
that I would at any moment be revealed for what it was I was.
And what was that? The old question: something now sunk,
deep in my seat, hardening between cushions,
indistinguishable as the grey chips

sloughed in the mess of the car: the space between
what is ordered, known, imperceptible in the dark.
It seemed easy to him, to know
and live his role, the job
a kind of calling, lost on me.

NISUS AND EURYALUS

> *...by heaven above*
> *And by the all-beholding stars above I swear*
> *He did but love his hapless friend too well.*
>   The Aeneid, book IX

In winter shut behind doors we'd shoot
contests from the foul line: a game
        of who could make

most in a row. Beginning again and again until
our arms ached, when dinner was called
        we walked back

to the common room as slow as we liked, practically
touching we were so close, jostling one another,
        gravel sliding underfoot.

I watched you in a game of pickup, moving between defenders,
cutting to the basket; it was like they were
        fumbling in the dark—

you made it look that easy, and I loved you, on the court
unstoppable. We swatted the ball,
        fluid in our moving

together. You caught me up into yourself cracking
jokes when I wanted to cry, taking me on walks
        or to the gym

to beat me again; you beat me at everything. It broke me
to lose you in the dark, in the brambles where I tried
        retracing my steps:

you, in the enemy's camp, captured or defected
I couldn't tell. I wept over leaving you alone to juke, or sprint,
        or cut whatever

way you needed to get yourself free. I couldn't hold you
then; I had a job to do, and watched you led
        away,

and girded myself in the shining helmet, running the path
to where our own forces lay, to deliver
      the message of war.

GUN

On the land
my brother palms me a revolver:
for wild dogs.

I go to work
hauling cut limbs in my white pick-up.
His morning's work

is clearing trees, mine
removal; I park my stack by the pile and kill
the engine.

I remember,
and grab the gun from the passenger's seat,
unholster it

and glints of light
squint my eyes. I tuck it in my pants
and hop to offloading limbs.

It looks good,
I think, with the butt stuck from my waistline,
crooked over the belt.

The pines all stacked in clumps
I want only to waste some yipping mutt;
I train to the treeline

the black muzzle
waiting for a shaded barreling figure
to cross my needled sight.

But no dogs,
and five idle bullets later
I join my brother in the clearing.

Loaded with tools
we set to finish, when from the dark
a wild cat darts,

blur of fur and claw,
my brother quick to aim, guns it down
only feet from freedom—

not cleanly, or enough,
so the bullet cleaves bone and lames
the twitching figure;

do you want to finish it?
I run with gun in hand, firing through the eye,
and ease the barrel back in place.

The strangeness
of the sound it makes
in the outcrop acoustics

like splintered wood,
ringing something final
in the thrill and shame of killing.

I wonder
at the gun's warmth, in the air
a whiff of gun powder,

the ease of sliding
into power, the snug grip affirming.
I hold the pistol

in my mind, perfect
the fit and weight. Each bullet
slides in chambers

like children
put to bed, tucked in steel;
honed and hopeful.

TEUCER

> *Never despair while under*
> *the guidance and auspices of Teucer*
>   Horace

Born to kill from far away, so first thing
out of high school he joins the navy, firing missiles

from submarines, never once missing—quick to laugh,
he was equally quick to start a fight. You'd see him in a bar,

picking pool cues to hurl across the room at the biggest
guy he could find, finding his mark, then ducking

behind monstrous Ajax and his seven-layered-oxhide shield.
After the war he met my father walking on the beach,

and together founded cities where all summer they would hold
bikini contests at the local bar, growing fat and old,

war stories swelling to legend in the telling and retelling.
He took me with him hunting once, to his usual spot. The dogs

moved through the woods, flushing deer from their beds.
I stood in a ditch by the road, shotgun enormous in my hands,

shaking in anticipation of the kill, and him beside me readied,
steadfast. We could hear the dogs as they advanced,

and frenzied movement of a prey pursued, but veering
suddenly, the chase ending elsewhere. I stood on the road relieved,

and laughed, and walked with him the whole day, glad
to be walking with him, hugging the silent tree line.

We returned to camp, slung guns draped over arms, taking
shit from others, but happier killless. In a dream I saw him

as he was once, loosing furious arrows, each shaft making a body,
sending souls of heroes howling to the marshes under Dis,

and behind the towering walls of Troy the wails of mourning started.

SKIPPING STONES

Sifting the river for the cool smoothness of stones
my brother and I judge in our hands the ones
shaped for skipping—

not too flat; heavy, but light enough to tip
the rills of water, popping nine or ten times,
enough to reach

the far shore. He arches his arm and throws
too hard—a great surface thud: one, two,
three times the water bowls its weight,

the fourth sucked low with a thwap that sinks it.
I more sideways whip mine: it sings
like taught strings plucked,

the twang leaping nine, ten, eleven times;
strikes a rock that clacks and sends it climbing
a far outcrop of trees.

My brother mutters something about *luck* and
next time, and I have to bring a hand to my mouth
to cover the smirk that says

what it needs to about luck or next time, standing
a little far off from him. I begin again
my search for rocks and hear behind me

my brother walking off the loss, his crunching
steps becoming quiet. Alone now with the river,
I thumb the stone

in hand, resting it in my palm like a trophy
I hurl thoughtlessly in one long arch over the water,
turning my back to wherever it lands.

THRALL

She walked as though the one hypnotizing stood
invisible, leading her through the train,
teaching her to call *spare change, spare change*;
the *a* in *change* ringing like enchantment.

Or maybe it was the strings
of a marionettist carrying
limbs outstretched where invisible cords
held her to the ventriloquizing voice.

It didn't seem cruel, this trance,
this stringed dance,
smiling as she moved through,
dodging book bags, brief cases.

Her eyes shone with something beyond fluorescence
or the work-lights in the dark beyond windows.
The one who held her, just out of reach,
beckoned, trailing, car by car—

beautiful, to watch her cradled
in the arms of some power, oblivious and happy;
metronomically clanking the change gathering
in the cup, without her knowing.

Would I hold out my hands to be pierced
and led away, or mind to be converted
to music? I thumb the rosary in my pocket.
The woman's gone, brought out

somewhere into the compartmentalized
beyond, paradise-out-of-mind;
the lights in our car flicker
and remain.

AJAX

He wasn't dumb, though when he spoke it was slow
and sounded like he was holding
fifty pennies in his mouth.

He had a face dogs didn't trust, but men
died for him, following his mad war cries
during football matches,

and whenever the kitchen sent up extra pudding.
His shield was always
where fighting was thickest.

You could trust him with violence
and kindness—once in the dorm he held me
in his massive arms

when nightmares kept me up, screaming in my bunk.
No god loved him,
but he never missed a service,

or skimped on offerings when the collection plate passed over his lap.
I can't say I liked him,
but I admired his brutal commitment

to keeping everything on the surface—if you were lying
he always knew, and made sure
everyone heard him call you out.

He had fits of schizophrenia, walking back and forth
screaming to himself and shaking.
It wasn't his violence

but his violence in love that scared me—
how once after laying down
his weapons he took me

by the throat and growled, *if you don't see people with love,
how do you see them?* and weeping,
threw me on the floor.

I still think of him, how he seemed so sure
of the truth that sent him wielding fury,
wild with killing;

and how at other times he got so close
I thought he would embrace me,
eyes wet and bewildered.

ENIGMA

A man on the platform shouts and shadowboxes, rubs hands
together like there's something he's plotting, some secret he's sputtering

in code about, laughing, the only one who understands,
lifting hands in victory, or swinging them wildly against unseen

opponents, vying in contest for whatever he's got; and his lousy jab
manages to keep away the curious or injurious, visible and invisible—

like Tommy Hearns, tall and lank, he spars with ghosts, swaggering
back and forth, reluctant to throw in the towel.

He comes at me as I'm bent over my bag and I straighten, looking
up to see he's not actually looking at me, but out beyond,

mouthing something, not about change or food, but absurdities
so I mumble a generic *sorry man* to get rid of him,

and he moves to others on the platform, bewildered in their newspapers,
walking out of sight as the train comes rolling in.

He appears, louder now, angry as if he were trying to make us understand
but has forgotten the language, his own code the only words he manages,

so he spends his days laboring to say what's eating at him,
squeezing out now and then some syllable in a surge,

swinging his limbs from subway poles like tree branches
and between the legs of strangers—right now it's *Bitch*

and *Nyquil*—the keys maybe, so that I could plug *Bitch*
and *Nyquil* into some decoding device and meaning would come

streaming through, and relieved, maybe he'd be able to stop
his wandering: known, finally, and heard like anyone else.

AT THE STOCKYARD

The best come first: females numbered for age, pregnant,
graffiti drooling down their flanks.
The old and worthless follow,

numberless: sad and dirty, skulking heads bent low,
needing no prodding. My mother leans in, *your
grandfather used to say, you can tell*

a lot about a farmer by how their cows look. And these, shrunken,
skittish, do tell. They'll fetch a few hundred bucks:
good for ground beef. Bad for breeding.

The bulls come last: knocking at the cage,
a few still with horns grown long, most with only stubs
barely visible above tufts of hair. They fight

bewildered in the arena, pacing, snorting, shaking great, black heads.
Goaded they enter, the silver prod threatening.
Made to prance, present now rump,

flanks, breasting now the crowd, pristine, strutting
slowly. Taking a beating for it. Most barely notice,
blasting back at the cage, making

the one with the whip jump back. Almost on their own time
they finally move into the long hall
where waiting trailers will take them away.

Even these will be broken, the wild auctioneer's voice
fluttering over loud speakers, incomprehensible;
acknowledging raised hands

from standing farmers who spit brown gobs in bottles
or on the floor next to slumped wives whose faces
vaguely fix somewhere in space.

After a while the ceremony becomes almost natural, sacred.
*Once, we sat on the first row and got shit all over us.
You get used to it.*

INHERITANCE

for Norburn Hyatt

Long step up the driver's seat
my grandfather makes
with less ease each new time—
teaching me to drive
he moves away
from one more responsibility.
We begin together:
check rotors, depress the clutch,
fire the ignition, start the blade's rotation;
slow clinking at first becoming
now a low hum
to the compliant engine.
He climbs down and waits,
standing small below himself.
Unsure in my seat,
I'm waved on by his hand
and mouthed command
to ease back on the gas,
follow my own tracks.
The smell of dew and cut grass
with each new pass
assures me looking at the pasture gate,
watching him
climb the house stairs—
the rotary churns,
cut hay slumped in heaps,
bowing in my wake.

TRACKS

West Main, and listening
to the bright bell sounds
announcing a train
and the lowering of the crossing guard across the road.

Poor blacks mingle
on the street together
near the placard to the great Peach Queen:
'Pride of the Southern Fleet.'

Rural whites on opposite corners
talk of weather, or the country,
run by Washington socialists;
portending doom.

The dance each does of not noticing
the other side, like lovers almost,
or siblings chased innocently from the scene,
the wreck they've made of the house.

The evening mimics
the pinstriped construction
of the Southern Railway—
centenarian now in the center of town.

The premier Peach Queen
carves through carrying its moon-white payload,
two dimensioned and
stately sharp in color.

What relief would these pictures give,
if like faces against glass they could mouth
the vowels that might soothe
this gut-nausea; history-sickness?

Ignorance like pressing feet,
sluggish in steel-toe; hands lifted in work,
in prayer; bodies tied to it, spikes
on a railroad.

QUILTS

Piled around the house were dozens of quilts,
enough to know grandparents lived next door.
They were hung up on walls, draped over beds

and the backs of chairs, stored in reserve in chests
and closets on the chance of some surprise visit, or random
kindness bringing casseroles or desserts casually by.

I've got one still, from childhood, moth eaten, hardly useful
then or now, as it barely reached over my feet—
warm enough at least, stitched with denim patches,

stuffed with wool. My brother has one like it, equally
mistreated, hoarded somewhere beyond my knowing, with knickknacks
stacked past understanding: some impulse or need lost in closets.

It was enough to make the house seem unreal, as if the quilts
were hung up to hem back time, or keep it out entirely;
each stitched pattern or patch sewn a kind of desperation,

something unsatisfied—making sure the kids stayed home
or young; to stop the door to sickness and death,
mastered in the shrewd nostalgic charm of antiques.

My grandmother's hands can't stitch the way they used to,
her eyes won't lead a thread through needles.
She walks alone through unreal rooms

where rag dolls slump, and knockoff tomahawks are gnawed
to nothing, rusted in closets; where quilts line
the papered walls like trophies, or accusations.

POSTS

We beat them in the wet ground; long necked green and white
the posts stand against the moldy wooden forerunners, shaped and

put up over half a century ago by my great-grandfather or maybe
one of his workers as he looked on (definitely looked on, at least:

the overseer's need so natural in my grandfather, who never
left me alone to mow, or saw, or put up fences until age kept him

away)—they're nearly falling over, held up by roots grown around them,
or stubbornness, inherited maybe from the same old men, if, like

I believe, the land becomes us, loved or ignored. We wrap strands
of barbed wire around the new posts, binding them to the old

like a crutch, down the line as necessary where age or trees have
toppled the grey, pocked columns. My mother and I in silent

rhythm take from the back of the four-wheeler each
upright length of ribbed metal, unspooling as we go more wire,

the joints in my hands ache from twisting, here and there bleeding
(I wear no gloves, too thick: less nimble than fingers). We re-learn

boundaries, remember to ourselves different lives' worth of time
spent walking these hills, the forest's view now bald in winter;

alone with hammer and step ladder, stumbling in brambles, cursing
occasionally, nearly nailing fingers (or once glancing my mother's

head, missing wildly from the ladder's step)—hemming back nature
with hammer and axe, with diligence. Warden, companion of silent miles.

LOGGING

They've torn from the back pasture entire acres.
I hear the machines working at my homecoming
down the long driveway. Invisible behind the barn

I hear them; the felling reminds me of years spent
riding the tree line looking for downed fences, trees
wobbled in hard wind, brought low in a hulk

of splintered trunk—but these, unnaturally
wasted, splinter by the dozen. Yellow metal
grips now the remains, moving out beyond the pines.

My mother turns. *They're clearing,* she says, and as if
anticipating something: *they've done a good job*;
made it look nice. I imagine through to the barbed wire

at the property line I remember rolling out
in labored lengths. Posting, re-posting, cutting, hammering;
taking the occasional metallic bite in what used to be

the thick of trees—long-grown oak, the few remaining
maples for years turning in their cycle
from spring's greens to brilliant

burnt sienna, vermillion, copper sunglow—
It paid for the new roof; how's your money
holding up? Your share's coming.

THE BOY AND THE MAP

He leaps on the seat and nearly kisses the hard plastic,
mouthing like he's sounding out the names,

though he isn't actually saying anything; and all along
he gapes, lips half-pursed so he looks

like a fish staring from the aquarium of the train
into the city, maybe wanting to swallow it, or just trying

to breathe in stops along colored routes, each line
of curiosity he drinks in, now making smacking noises

with his lips, open and closed, so I'm sure he's a fish
sidled up next to me, shoving his way between

passengers so his father has to talk him down; but the boy
keeps drinking in the map, so close I wonder

if he can actually make out the names at all,
or if it even matters, his hunger for place

so much neater—the world set before you like a meal,
and all you have to do is move over close enough to gobble it up.

GRADE SCHOOL MYTHOLOGY

Teaching this morning the myth of Orpheus
and a mapping of the underworld,
but rain has made the kids into a downpour

of distraction crafts can't focus—raising
the poster paper above their heads they stand,
shaking to make thunderstorms.

One in the corner hums to the thrum of rain
on windows. Others run back and forth
between supplies and painted poster paper

depicting different hells, different visions:
floods of purple, orange, and dark blue,
rivers fed by the deep and violet Styx,

bounding over stenciled borders
into the blank space between Tartarus
and the Blessed Fields, where love might

slip unnoticed into the margins of the world.
For homework they were told to practice
walking ahead of their loved ones for fifteen minutes

without looking back. One girl tells us
"I thought my mom might take some
unexpected turn and I'd be lost…" *Am I dreaming?*

Orpheus must have wondered at his joy turning
to panic like a child's looking back for one
damning second at love rounding the corner.

THROUGH THE PEEPHOLE

I thought it might be sex noises: high pitched
squeals, sounds of banging furniture,
and then higher, louder, a different shout
outside the door: two children, nine or ten,
a boy and girl playing tag, up and down
the hotel hallway in their pajamas, giggling,
hitting each other, disappearing again,
this time into their own room next door.
More slamming, and they're back at it,
kneading the red carpet with bare feet.

It's lovely, this unexpected running, barefoot
in pajamas down halls; a welcome disturbance
where sleepers grumble in their numbered
beds, away from games played; straining
at the door to keep in view something
daring disruption, distorted in distance.

DANCE

At the dance for incoming sixth graders
I was wearing my favorite
buttoned-up Hawaiian shirt.

Prepubescent, glum, and sparsely pimpled,
late in catching on to the make-out craze
of my popular classmates, I thought clothes

could pluck me from my perpetually being only present,
like a desk, or set of lockers. That night I was plucked,
from obscurity into the ridiculous, standing,

a floral backdrop to the white-washed cinderblock
cafeteria walls, mingling I'm sure with others
similarly visible, maybe swaying back and forth,

trying without success to catch the eyes
of Hyatt Kirwin, the little girl from history
class, designated Spartan with myself

in the Grecian city-state contest our teacher held,
winning together I forget exactly which prize.
She stood sheltered in a swarm of girls,

and after an hour or so I stirred my valor,
shuffling to the center of the hive where eyes
glared over the emblazoned blue and yellow leis.

Disarmed, I stutter-stepped my speech
and blurted something about dancing
I can't now remember; and Hyatt pronouncing

no sent me beaten from the field. I remember
with bitterness the foolishness of it,
but mostly the girl who'd whipped me

in all my gathered battle vigor. But, then again,
maybe it isn't enough to just remember—
what I imagined as contempt maybe

her embarrassment at my clumsy, swaggering
attempt to woo; maybe in the equal confusion
and distress of adolescence we crashed, headlong,

nobody's fault—the casualty only of chemicals
working fever in our brains. Maybe it's time
to call a truce with the old hurts,

The difficulties of who I am and was: unkind
as often as kind—enough to consider
recompense for any offense

I may have taken. Maybe in the blur of distance
we can call it quits, this business of blame,
and climbing from the wreck

of memory there will be understanding
between who we were and are today;
and wounded, we'll hobble to the middle

like a kind of dance, partners reaching from the strobe-
lit, Hawaiian-shirt past into the present. Forgetful,
we'll touch hands, lost in the music of it all.

DUCKLINGS

for David Ferry

I met some ducklings on their way to somewhere
on the river: three stopping by me calling

to them, my sporadic quacking likely strange
but curiously stopping by

on their way hurriedly anywhere as long as it was
forward, maybe lost and looking

for other ducks, maybe paddling away from other ducks.
Who can know? Only they were very eager in their searching

maybe a little desperate to be stopping by me
on the river speaking poorly their mother tongue.

Was it company they needed? I must have confused them
saying over and over the same phrase so they felt sorry

for me, big broken duck who had forgotten how to speak.
Paddling quickly along they passed me by,

swept along in the current of words,
searching for someone else to talk to on the river.

WORDS LIKE OURS

In the dark of the bar we were the words we were saying
to one another, maybe not fully
aware of what we were saying

while it was being said. What was spoken between us
became what we were to each other
in the downpour

of words that kept us together, drowning
what was being said
at other tables

between others maybe like us, lost to the vocables
that meant being unalone awhile, even
if all we managed

was lost speech, broken to bits by later, half-
remembrances, drinking-in what
was bound to be said.

In the barroom it was raining what was said,
and maybe we held some of it, cupped in hands,
or mouths shaped in O's,

catching what we could, soaked in hair and running
over skin. Later we could still wring
on the floor

whatever might be left from what was said: drops, halved
and quartered, endlessly discovered, soaked up
to be drained and lost again

in the dark of the dried-up bar talk, waiting for later others
who would be saying before long
words like ours.

PICTURE OF US

for Rachel Anthony

It was my birthday and we stood—you, beautiful, youthful; me, spectacled,
unable for the life of me to comb my hair correctly—in the lobby of a
hibachi steak house. After, I remember we were all over each other in the
cramped cabin of my truck, in a field, on the deck of your pool.
I don't remember you crying, though maybe you wanted to.

And I wasn't helping, being myself. We'd weather a few more months'
worth of disasters together: I took and used what you gave and after, always
remorse. Rinse, repeat. It's funny now, sort of—nothing we could make last,
at least. I keep the picture as a bookmark in Auden's *Collected Poems*, placed
now facing 'Lullaby,' so it's like the two of us are reading poems together—

lay your sleeping head, my love, human on my faithless arm—Auden knew
what affection costs us in headache, heartache; ours no different, so it's
fitting to leave us there, in his care. We do look happy, standing by the lobby
couches, against each other bright in the camera flash, under lights,
my class-ringed finger gripping your shoulder, yours my waist.

The other day I saw you got engaged, saw the picture of the two of you
closer than us, faces touching, smiles honest. He looks nice, and you, happy.
But between us: what we said, how we suffered, it's all still there,
though better as memory (we'd have been very unhappy together);
better like this: posed always in affection, in the dark of leftover words.

HELEN

I was afraid, looking from the plains, up to battlements
where she stood, remembering my place in line

behind Hector Breaker of Horses, Sarpedon Built
Like a God, and Paris Boy Toy of Aphrodite.

It's not that I'm bad looking, I'm not. I've got money,
and am fairly competent with sword and javelin.

I ran the mile in under five minutes in high school,
and have read Derrida; can talk about him a little.

Everyone knows she's pretty, devoted to the gods,
and that's enough for every weekend warrior

to claim her for their own. But she wears chastity
like a gun, to discourage thugs and suitors.

Wild, she made men into murderers, and would burn
us all out of our homes, bolting like bewildered animals.

I loved her, and would have killed, Greek or Trojan,
to be up there with her in the sun, aloof and royal on the walls.

GLASS

for Mark Doty

I join you in the wordless hospital room
where tv static settles on your body, curled
under blankets, your head only
appearing above covers.

Maybe you really are asleep this time.
I'm allowed my book, resting on the table. I watch
some muted, made-for-tv remake of Cinderella.
I have to leave

my pen with the nurse, so I use a crayon, scratching
notes on one of your half-colored pictures
I can't decipher. You should be sleeping
in your own bed,

with the family that wanted you until they didn't.
You should be home, away from the lonely
shuffle of doctors, microwaved meals, and lights
out at nine. All done,

fallen through, who knows how?
When news broke you swung madly, broke
windows and swallowed the glass, settling
in yourself something unsettled,

leaving only this strangeness behind, silence;
your barely breathing figure heaped beneath sheets.
A week ago, readying for bed
you called to me

doing head checks on the others, unusually
bright: *I'm going to be adopted.* You hadn't
put more than a few words together
in months, and all at once,

a revelation: *do you think they'll like me?*
Standing bedside to your triumph, I leaned into
my assurance: *they're lucky to have you.*
You smiled,

and with a hand rubbed, down from the crook
of your elbow, each scar along your arm. Now
I think I've come to it, wondering a while after you
there, like a kind of nothing,

how you took into yourself the pressure, sand
and sheen, the sheet unbearable,
light splintering in refracted fragments, cutting
a shaft of clarity

irrational and nearly fatal, but resembling sense,
your answering maybe for good the question
in your blood; having found at last
a place, belonging

to the elements, this reduction of form
a child's idea of purity: easing
at last into blankness,
pure reflection.

PRESENCE

We exchange pressure, pulsing like code:
hands squeezing or fingers tapping on arms,
wrists, the backs of palms; glances met
with grins, modest looks down or back
to the mass: the priest's arms sweeping
overhead like a swimmer's, down,
holding the God-crumbs, my own hands holding
hers, rubbed with thumb and forefinger
like a nervous tick: *are you still there?*
She blushes, receiving the kiss I give
in the exchange of peace. I grip waist and thigh,
felt through dress and stockings; hoped for,
to be felt over again. We kneel apart,
as if to spend our thoughts on God,
somewhere the soul groping for presence.
Eyes closed, I feel a hand snake through
the hoop of my arm, draped over the pew.
The tips of her fingers drift down to the crook
of my elbow and grip as if dipping in the circuit
I've made in the closed fold of my hands.
I open my eyes to the priest standing
like the model of steeples we made
with our bodies as children—hands raised,
coupled overhead, the held host shown
to us gripping one another lightly now,
blushing, maybe in shame or fear,
releasing our grips until only the memory of touch
hovers above the surface of our skin.

QUOTIDIAN

Are you back in the south of France? Julia. I remember
the title of your poem, when you shared it for the first time

I had to look it up. *Quotidian.* There were other words, something
on the page about bedsheets, rumpled and drawn out

in the sun; dog kisses, or steam from morning coffee
condensing on your chin—and that may be all

I remember. *Quotidian.* Everyday. Ordinary.
You'd cobbled together the awkward cut stones,

images of mornings alone, and I've taken the word,
may have even made up the rest—what I would say

about your life. Just ordinary. Are you
back in the south of France, or maybe Brooklyn, still

in the loft you praised (were you praising?) as daily; ordinary
only? *Quotidian.* I split my own dumb rocks for paving

whatever it was about you might have thought was only
merely everyday: (dis)praising the house, keeping the plant alive,

the sheets, coffee. I hobble through details and remember
you only in the fiction of memory—somewhere in the south of France,

or posed in sunlight on sheets maybe needing changing,
or plants needing watering, or coffee needing drinking.

Quotidian. From Latin, coming down without much difference
to us directly. I can pin it down, ringing like Georgics

so there's something in it like labor. Ploughing,
keeping bees. Straightforward, down the line to you and me

a couple millennia in the history of what's only merely daily.
Julia. There's so much more to say that isn't in the coffee

you've probably finished, wiping from around your mouth the accumulated
wet, or in sheets we'd never share now tumbling in the dryer,

or the plant maybe dead or forgotten in a move away from Brooklyn—
a move home, maybe, or back to the south of France.

FEET

I ask the man taking up three seats—bags piled
around him, his life of lottery tickets,

candy bar wrappers, indecipherable scraps—
I ask if he wouldn't mind moving over.

He grips the bags to slide them down
and as he moves I see his feet

in what must have been nice sandals once,
a size or two too big, duct-taped at the straps—

his feet, poor things, the grime congealing
into tar, chipped here and there, stretching

to his calves like a sock, toenails all broken.
When Saint Francis heard the leper ringing

in the night, he embraced him. And Jesus washed
the feet of fishermen and whores, stooping

over the basin, the stink sloshing
in the bucket, remains of what he'd laved off.

Poor creature, is there no one left to love,
to wash you? It wasn't me getting to my knees,

the water from my bottle emptied
on the young man's feet, scrubbing the blood

and pus; kissing them even, like Francis,
begging forgiveness, or like Magdalene

weeping over Jesus's feet, with her hair
mopping up dust from across Galilee.

Who sinned, this man or his parents,
that he was born this way?

He combs his beard with black fingernails, preening
in the window; lights in the tunnel pass

his face watching me in the glass,
grinning or snarling.

JESUS'S KNEES

Considering the smallness of the chapel, the crucifix is enormous,
Christ looking like he might have been carved from driftwood—
he would have liked that, *The Son of Man*

has no place to lay his head—and I swear from where he's hanging
it's like he's staring at me, so when I find myself
wondering if the beautiful

young woman kneeling across the aisle might be single,
I look back and catch his eyes (ridiculous, blue eyes),
nearly squinting,

in consternation maybe, directing me with the same gaze to his
hands, feet planted around the darkened nail head. But it's these
knees I think about most:

rubbed darker than the rest of the wood so his falling on the road
seems something accounted for in the making,
bruised and filthy,

in my mind shredded on rocks and bloodied, so I can't help thinking
how I want to scrub them clean, sand them
down to the white underneath.

Golden driftwood! What savior made in your image could hang
for so long this way? I've seen the nails a thousand times,
but these knees,

with what devotion to the minutiae of pain they surprise, terrify—
further darkening as the light is put out and I'm left
beneath their suffering landscape.

EUCHARIST

Stepping in line there's only ever trying to focus
against the kneeler's creaking back into position,
or my eyes roving over to the woman next to me,
the one in front, shapely even in modesty—
focused on what I'm here for, the Christ-loaf,

ineffable mystery, God-in-bread, and all that.
I talk myself into what matters, eyes above heads,
up to the crucifix, Macaroon-brown Jesus, shaggy
and muscled, lit from all sides, the shadowed undercross
shaping a figure which looks to be supporting

the Lord's weight, like he's being kept there,
not by the nails, but by this devilish little silhouette
upholding the scene. Occasionally I look down
at the rubber slips I wear, stupidly uncomplimenting
my khaki shorts and collared shirt, now taking

as the object of meditation my own feet,
the carpet pattern, the slim calves
of the woman ahead of me in line.
Coming closer to the moment
and the man, robed and placing in mouths

what I'm supposed to know as matter-of-fact
as I do my feet, the carpet, this lady's calves.
*Oh, Son of God, bring me into Communion
this day with your mystical supper*, and forgive me
for all the things I've done with my tongue.

The Deacon mumbles *body of Christ* and jabs
the wafer at the waiting gape of my mouth,
missing with fingers so the thing drops,
fluttering to the floor, and for a moment we pause
in the shock of it all before he scrambles

to pluck it up again—Jesus grounded, the unforgivable
faux pas—and returns again, sliding the tainted
wafer behind others, offering another, fresh host.
All I can do is revive my embarrassment for him, rolling
slightly my eyes, nodding my furrowed forehead to save face,

as if to say, *can we get it right this time?* And receiving
the host with gratitude for getting the hell out of there,
back to my place in the pews; creaking kneeler,
lady's calves, and the still-shadowed, shaggy-bearded macaroon
Christ, looking down now at me in particular munching

on His body, my trying feebly but failing
to remember what to pray, only thinking of leaving outright,
grabbing my shit and gone like Peter shuffling from his place
in the crowd, the Lord's eye's roving him over;
and from somewhere, a distant rooster croaking sunrise.

POLITES

after the painting by Jules Lefebvre

Polites lies in bloodless rest: boyish,
as if death had come,
sleepwalking in the night—

but for the heel of Pyrrhus
and Priam gripped in grief,
betraying the scene of war,

he might have been an athlete dying young,
in bed, or at his games; instead
he's painted in the dying city,

left to wonder at, and mourn restlessly.
Fire and fury, practiced savageries;
a blessing killed Polites first—

blessing he was born a man
and prince of Troy,
escaping rape and slavery,

the abiding nightmare—a blessing
to die so, under the gaze of his gods
and at his father's feet.

SHOES

My father would line up for inspection rows of shoes:
his, my mother and brother's, all on the carpet.
I'd walk the line,
inspecting each pair,

looking, looking, and when
unsure, would reach down to feel
for the curve, left or right,
my father all along nodding.

I remember his overlarge shoes in my hands,
fingering the tongue,
laces, tread; hands remembering
his lessons,

and the patience when he taught me, standing near
until I matched them all.
This morning I put my shoes on in the dark,
feeling for the curves

rounding left, right, stretching the laces,
lifting the tongue. He stands
nodding over me now like the dark I sit in,
waiting for me to get it right.

POCKETS

We've emptied the dead man's closet, shoes in rows
gone: to charity, one or two I kept (boots,
loafers a size too big). Shirts tossed, formal

jackets (two tuxedos!), coats, scarves, hats
and windbreakers. But in every pocket stuffed in bunches
there were paper towels. He hadn't kept a handkerchief

in years, so we found, ball after ball, these wadded
white lumps. I found one the other morning
in a jacket I'd saved, white ruffled clump

I remember he'd used, sneezing in the truck, or offered
after lunch—crumbs, mustard staining the edges
of my mouth, beard when I was older—and refusing

never stopped him asking, pulling a wad out silently,
motioning with a wrist thrust across table
or truck console, sly smile or chuckle

at my waving him off, using instead my sleeve or hand.
Later, deeper in backpacks we found and arranged
on the floor his readiness—tape, rope,

first-aid kits filling plastic bags, extra hooks packed
for fishing trips, maps, ponchos, crackers
and Vienna Sausages—he planned for both of us,

was willing (wanted) to share—spaces he held
for what was needed: my grandfather, ready
always with a kindness tucked in pockets.

HIDING PLACES

I would sink my hands in the deep of a purse,
plunging wrist-deep in dark; fingering

leather crevices sewn shut with silk stitches,
or buttoned, clinched with bronze and silver

figures etched in miniature: anchors, flowers,
nonsensical symmetry of circles.

I'd run fingernails in bladed searching
like a figure skater, or pop with effort stubborn snaps

to break into the deep insides. I'd sift
through woven strands of crystal gilded

in sockets, snaking threads on wrists and fingers,
sunk and squirming in the cool metal, lifting swarms

of gold, letting fall again in piles left slumped,
groped now and then by my hands

shutting reluctantly their brightness out of sight.
Shoes too, stoic in rows, I'd shove roughly over hands

to the tips of toes, clapping together heel and palm,
gloved in pink pumps, black flats; sliding fingers

through loops of sandals—all returned at the sound
of father bumping furniture, mother

creaking floorboards. I'd hide in the folds of clothes,
sneaking along the back, brushing lightly

dresses draped in dry-cleaning plastic,
or pantsuits rough against my skin; nightgowns

and blouses blown back at my grabbing handfuls
stopping my fall—heard, certainly,

rummaging always for some unplumbed treasure,
some fact of my only knowing.

AGAMEMNON

He blustered with the best of them
and commanded the boy's dorm,
marching in line behind the last,

always shortest and loudest in a crowd.
He was King of the faculty softball team
(and it pleased him, firing a line drive

just past my glove in right field,
cheering as he rounded third base).
He was changeable like luck

and happily stepped on anyone
he caught whimpering outside his office.
He wasn't beyond consolation

(he was eloquent and often wrong),
but his kindness always stank like a favor,
so you never knew the score,

or even what game you were playing.
He was that good, and still is, probably—
Emperor of a one-room apartment;

divorced (Clytemnestra left him in bed
with the school psychologist), though no doubt
managing to bully someone, maybe the newbies

in the cafeteria at the 8pm A.A. meeting.
I can still see him, glittering in bronze
atop his chariot, yoking his team of stallions

(second only to the pair Achilles owned):
The Unbowed, The King of men—and I become
the green boy again, pissing himself on the shores of Troy.

DAD'S NAPS

He took daily, with the regularity of ritual,
hours-long naps, horizontal meditations.
Never much of a church man, he'd prostrate himself
on the altar of couch cushions,

always at midday, so the drone of *Matlock, Murder
She Wrote,* or *Columbo* rang from Sext to None
the old man's keeping of the *horae.*
What became of me,

lapsing from view into who can remember what? Play,
certainly, the muted cajoling of quieter toys
(to wake him was to rouse what was godly, sacred;
the force of his wrath).

I likely watched for a while Andy Griffith ambling
in the unbelievability of his role as attorney;
muted jazz notes of the opening credits
ringing even now

as I stretch to recreate each scene of my encounter
with those afternoons, dad splayed
and snoring, and me, maybe lost
in backyard brambles,

or scoring on myself, H.O.R.S.E., the driveway
rim reverberating those solo performances.
And now? How I spend each midday
imitating him

in one way I wouldn't mind (the man died
a drunk), napping on the couch at midday.
How much have I lost of those hours,
captive to his worship,

and how much is left still to recover, in the effort
maybe to take what was good in his absence
and credit him with, what? If not love,
at least warmth.

OLD MAN

I'm wondering for the first time in who-knows-how-long
at my father's barrel-chested posture, his widow's peak,

his strong jaw pitched forward into frame—
dead now only a few-years-shy of two decades,

and on the occasion of what would have been
his sixty-ninth birthday, he still baffles me.

How are there no pictures online, when everything's
up for grabs, to be searched and looked over?

Not a single one, from his obituary even;
only a tombstone and picture

of his nearly-equally-long dead mother.
And why do I call him old man

when I only ever called him dad,
and he stopped aging at least ten years

before anyone could call him old?
Why (I could probably guess this one)

after so long does his best friend, my godfather,
still message me every January 28th—

"Happy Birthday Bill Kulseth"—a man
I wouldn't wish alive again even if I could.

More questions: why is it a memory seems to age
when the one we're remembering hasn't

been around for years? Is it that, as we grow
we remember differently, maybe nurturing

some new sympathy or hatred, aging
past the lived memory into something else,

some vision we make for ourselves?
Maybe that's it. Don't get me wrong,

I don't hate the old man anymore, only,
I know if he were alive to meet his sixty-ninth birthday,

I wouldn't have remembered still,
and there'd be nothing

prompting these questions leading nowhere,
that don't matter anyway,

but which offer a break from maybe what's saddest:
how like a *thing* he's become for me,

just another numbered square on the calendar.
Battle of Waterloo, June 18th;

first public radio broadcast, December 24th;
invention of the fountain pen, May 25th;

the Old Man's birthday, January 28th,
followed hard by the anniversary of his death, February 20th—

facts of history, casually recalled, agreed upon,
and forgotten once again.

BEATING

> *after Robert Hayden*

My father cups his hand in the way we were taught
to cup our hands to make a stroke through water,
or how we made instruments

with our mouths by taking hands and clapping
together in front of our mouths rounded in O's,
the wooden sound something similar to the hard

and measured smacking he puts me through.
But it's never too much, even when taking clippers
to the yard I cut the bamboo he never uses, thick

shoot I think might hurt less than the wiry others.
To scare me he keeps it hanging in his shed
where maybe half the time threat turns into real beating.

It's no purge, no sweating hunched over
to catch his breath after. It's a spanking,
preceded in this way by the unbelievable

its gonna hurt me more than you, and followed
by embrace—his walking through of ritual,
like something he thinks all fathers do.

But it was summer when I must have done
something terrible which I've forgotten, when
my mother laid on thick threats of my father's

coming home to use the posed bamboo shoot, or cupped
hand, or gnarled leather belt whose buckle I still hear
in the fidgeting to have it off—and I took from drawers

all the underwear I had, layering until my pants
bulged and I waddled all day waiting for the spanking
that never came—he just sat me down, padding

bunched against couch cushions, riding up my legs,
sweating and red in however many pairs I wore.
It was over. The fear, he said, was enough.

MARTHA AND TOOTER

Wedged between a pair of stairway pillars
in the backyard of our house,
a few yards from the beehives and a high fence,
in the middle of an untended garden,
my mother built a chicken coop
where two hens clucked pettily over corn,
produced few eggs, and painted the coop white.

She named them *Martha* and *Tooter*,
after her mother and aunt,
and they bickered like old ladies
but lived comfortably
between the stairway pillars
a few yards from the dangerous bees,
lost in a tangle of garden brambles.

An inside joke, my mother never
called them chickens, only
Martha and *Tooter*: and the longer
both pairs lived the more alike they became,
clucking and scraping at corn or gossip—
which led to confusion one afternoon
when through a message I learned

how *Martha and Tooter were eaten by coyotes*,
who leapt one night over the high fence,
past hordes of swarming bees
in a mesh of garden weeds
under stairs and two concrete pillars,
and burrowed under chicken wire to enjoy
two old birds sleeping unruffled in their beds.

BARN

Farmers from the pre-electric centuries mixed
skimmed milk, lime, linseed oil, and iron oxide

to make the paint so prominent on barn walls, keeping
heat from hay-cramped lofts; left wide-spaced slats

to soothe their guts in summer months.
And this one's no different, bright red,

gaping wide spaces between timbers.
For years it was like this, when the barn

was used as more than storage for old tools
and rolls of barbed wire, or as a haven for mice

and wasps' nests pock marked on rafters. If asked,
what might it say? What stories tell?

If open-mouthed cracks could croak its past
and spill more than hay (who knows how many

years old and stale) what secrets would tumble
from the days my grandfather spent breaking

horses as a boy, proud and whipped
with broom handles? Or my great-grandfather's

labored heaving in baling season? Or my own
searchings for rusted treasures, taking

in my small hands axe and hammer, some tool
of lost use? Propped in rickety persistence,

barns like these number in the hundreds, relics
of hillside miles, yawning into whatever

future will keep them (having outlived cattle, horses,
and men). The tin roof glints a day's-breadth of light,

winking, maybe, at something understood,
some secret hinted at, and overlooked.

HARVEST

    for Lane Hyatt

That season was hard in drought
and the strawberries
my father planted suffered worst.

We were sent off to fetch pine needles
hauled in trucks, settling
the straw under each patch;

it kept them, heads above mud
when rain would fall and soak the field
and swell the speckled reds.

But no rain that season
made our gathering and trouble-taking
fruitless. So our father sent us

to dig ravines out from the creek so water
pooled-in deep. He took when we were done
horse and plow and ranged

trenches to where the patch sat dry and low.
Later we gathered rocks to stop
the water in its flow, to govern

he said, what ran into the fields.
When the rocks were in place, he'd walk
from lane to lane, lifting up,

at his farmer's discretion, each rock,
loose just enough to let the strawberries
drink, then stopper it back.

Till midnight most nights that dry season
my father in place would stand
or walk along the patches,

*and lift and weigh each one's turn to drink,
replacing when he would and moving on
till all had had their fill—*

My grandfather on the front porch
relates these facts of my inheritance—
of men, the ones like his father,

whose work kept a family fed:
*I'll never cease to be amazed;
all that was done here,*

he nods to the lower field, where
cattle graze lazily, and the heat
of the day has browned the cut grass

where no strawberries grow;
the lane where his father paced
running like a vein through the field.

BROODY

for Annie, eaten by foxes

Twice daily I carry her from the coop:
ruffled-red, puffy Buff Orpington
squatting relentlessly on her nest.

My mother says she's broody, some instinct
of breeding—sitting all day without food,
dying sometimes in their self-restraint.

She stakes her claim on the middle nest box,
alone in the dark; would slumber comfortably
but for my routine plucking her plump body,

placing her on the corn pile. She gives back low
grumbling clucks muffled in her plume,
disheveled and annoyed, with effort moving

to water, lets on she's learned a lesson,
then once I've turned away, waddles quickly
back inside the barn to haunt the empty nest.

I understand the impulse to brood
on dead things, or whatever it might be—
neither alive or dead, but only

with potential to live and die:
those never-quickened impulses,
germs of thought which force a mulling over,

so these sedentary days seem only natural.
Hunger, restlessness, do we choose
what drives us, or only ride to the end

a wave of fervor: our obsessions,
whatever is unhatched requiring all of us,
time and stillness, a sitting discipline.

ACHILLES

Huddled in a ring, we break to our formations,
equal in gear and stature, readied in line
and waiting for the whistle's signal to work.

He is known by all from the beginning,
comfortable in place behind the lines—
his inevitable charge surprises no one.

He wraps himself around the ball as if it were
Patroclus, alive again, and frail; we wrap
ourselves around him, charging in a line.

It's been written: his grace in battle unmatched,
his skill and poise, the way he moved—
I watch him carry the ball up and down

the field, vaulting like a dancer; feel him in practice
whipping his body into mine, shoulders lurched
in my chest like a weapon some god made.

And his weapon sang under stadium lights, built
to steal the breath from whomever he met,
cascading to the end like the sea poured out

on our enemies. We cheered him,
but he was deaf to everything except the urging
of Patroclus, whom he could not save,

held in his hands, where even rushing to the end
of the field was no safety for his love, nor rest
for the goddess-born, held on our shoulders.

HECTOR

He was always towel-whipping boys in the locker room,
His crew all howling when he caught one off guard,
stripped to their skivvies, backs to the wall.

Or standing in left field he'd bat fly balls in the sun
nearly breaking my glasses when I'd miss with my mitt.
But he was the coach's kid, beloved of the gods.

Thus strode to the plate keen Achilles, swift runner
from two towns over, his weapon glittering:
bat forged by the gods to drive the ball over walls,

lighting every pitch past poor Hector's ears. I smiled
behind the Breaker of Horses sweating on the mound,
whiffing balls outside the strike-zone

so every Achaean walked-in runs and drove
our armies back behind the walls. Dead
he came to me in a dream, warning of the anger

of the gods and clashing steel, Troy on fire; his face
disfigured with tears, clothes torn and dirtied with chalk
and infield clay. He loomed for a while holding

out to me our trophies, imploring me to rise, take
up arms and carry them elsewhere, away.
I rolled over, snoring, and let the vision fade.

CHARITY

Walking down 45th and Lex. toward Grand Central
I spot splayed across the subway steam grate
a man soaking up heat on the first cold morning of fall.

Not a bad idea, I say to a friend, the guy still within earshot
but passed out, or seeming so, wrapped in steam
dreams. *If I were homeless*, yada yada yada

something about the ingenuity of street people.
Not ten feet further a woman's sitting on the concrete stoop
under a storefront window, leaning on a release valve:

she's got bags of who knows what stacked around
and beneath her like a throne; all made up,
she's like a child's idea of royalty: thick pink eye-shadow,

pink lipstick, pink everything, and these fake jewels draped
from her neck and wrists. *Seems like a lot of work*, I say;
at least she's trying to keep up appearances.

What are these annotations I feel the need to lay on
the margins of their lives like approval? Later I slip a Metro
card into some guy's hands asking for a swipe. He turns

through the stile and mouths, *God bless*—I point and nod,
lips pursed like I'm relating some shared predicament;
like this guy's my brother, and what wouldn't I do to help my brother?

REFLECTION

Gold-leafed in light, like candy wrappers bunched and spent,
or like the ticket I'd seen slipped a thousand times

from the Wonka bar, held and blinked at in the disbelief of it all,
he grips a fistful of condoms and offers them boldly

to a stranger who smiles (laughs even, a real laugh),
waving her hand in refusal. He shrugs, reaching into his black

bag to lift an enormous bottle, grimacing a swig, returning it to jostle
with others, arm wavering, sloshed. How like a kid,

his swagger, taking public swigs—the bottle, his tilting-
to-the-ceiling of it like my own at his age toasting the bare sky,

wincing when the harshness hit my lips,
groping the table for chaser, with each later sip willing

the stinging liquid. And the rubbers he held—
shoved roughly out of sight, gold becoming the brown

of Bourbon, the laminate wrapper as hard as glass.
I didn't use them my first time, didn't know how,

couldn't buy them if I wanted. The first unwrapped for me,
I couldn't make out the brand in the dark,

the sleekness foreign, sterile, my pleasure all power
trading places until the inevitable, numbed spasm.

I watch the young man bargaining dumbly with the uninterested world,
pulling out one last time the bottle, clumsily unscrewing the top,

talking again, his words coming like an echo from my own mouth,
our reflection mirrored in the closing doors.

RAISING THE HUNLEY

They've rigged a cage to lift and hold the thing, cradled
in ratchet-straps and swaying as it breaks water, rusted, barnacled.
The camera cuts

now and then to men and women in jump-suits working
the rig; others toast and hug. It's so much smaller
than I thought,

so I can't help but think of its final crew hunched
over hand cranks, blind with sweat in the cramped chamber,
tired, dying.

And all around smiling crowds halloo the remorseless lump,
barely recognizable coming out of the waves,
brought up at last

into a circle of fifty or so skiffs that sit on the still sea.
Most hoist the stars and bars, strung up on masts
or makeshift flag poles.

I get it, why we were so happy then. I was nine
and never thought of what it all meant,
only excitement,

and what the boats looked like from shore, hundreds
it seemed, and each one, I was eager to think, might have been
the one that did the job

so I could tell everyone at school, *I saw it! I saw them
pulling it out of the water!* I remember too my father, raising up
two fists full of steel,

indicating thickness of submarine walls on the one
he served on: nuclear powered, enormous; *The Hunley*
shriveled in comparison.

I think now how silly it is, this raising of the three-times-failed
submarine that miscarried more often than any blowing-out-of-the-water
of the enemy was worth;

proud and delirious men buried alive, watching water
spill through raked metal, filling the compartment.
Just a matter of time.

Despite it all the crowds still cheer to see the brown body
finally brought home, sun behind clouds
breaking like a thought:

the Confederate wreck a kind of triumph, even as inside
old bones are pitched and broken,
trapped in the dark.

NEW JERUSALEM

He pronounces the *bur* in *burn* with deep
affected grumbling; the kind you'd use
to stutter out the sound for the feeling of cold,
stretching the syllable

to the thrum of two or three. Not cold,
but a sizzling like singed skin,
his affectation a little heavy handed
in the force of his telling

of the siege of Jerusalem—*when Roman
armies under the command of Titus
surrounded the city, leveled its temple,
and burned the remains.*

He dramatizes in speech so well
the city's fall you'd think it was Josephus
negotiating the performance
with personal extravagance,

but the old priest's homily is nothing
I remember anything of save
his recital, the rhetoric impressive,
horrible—

the fear he stirs something like that lingering syllable:
a people huddled in the dim church,
fortified weakly against night and cold,
cobbled like stones together,

afraid of the dark and some numberless force imagined
outside their walls; the vague encroaching
threat: faceless and felt like air
burning, burning.

LEAVING TROY

for Wando High School, Class of '09

We sift the beach with shifting feet,
each in our separate selves, each
a wreck over leaving
the work of killing
we've come to love. All done,
and how to put this feeling into words? We won.

The loot sorted, we dispense
the still smoking embers of our friends.
I grip the ash shaft and remember well
princes I sent with a quip
and a spear tip
to hell.

Under walls and on beaches,
savage like furies
we emerged on shore,
glittering in our gear
and eager like meat
for the grinder.

We knew as much as this: war
becomes us, and each
to each saluting on the beach
can only stand now and wonder,
if we were different than we are,
could we be happy?

The lost still have some part
in our lives, and dead I know
they feel it too, the waste—
so cock-sure, and for what?
Some girl, loot
even the sea will forget.

I feel it, bone-weariness
standing battle-clad
in glints of light: the Great Host
of who's left—we're alive
at least, content with what we've done,
though it feels like ruin.

HORSES

> *And so the Trojans buried Hector breaker of horses*
> Iliad, Book XXIV

They spent the day breaking horses,
My grandfather and his brother—
his brother the natural
with a broom handle, applied
with backwoods magic
only slightly sinister.
They'd finished the job
in an afternoon, walking
different beasts from the barn.
Climbing up, they posed
for the picture posted
years later beside grandchildren
holding caught bass, snapping
turtles—the brothers brave
in black and white, animals
calm under their weight,
nosing the air, curious maybe
at their new condition.

Maybe dying is like that, walking
from the bounded dark,
unaware of what you were
only moments before:
no longer your own, following
after one another
into a new greenness,
led by powers only
slightly sinister, from some
final shelter into the sun,
posed and smiling.

They're all dead, men
and horses, greying to their end
like the photograph, faster
than our remembrance
of them. The barn's here,

and I remember when
my grandfather took me
to the place where they
walked in reluctant horses
and walked them out again.
He would pause and smile
as the sun caught him up
and he entered somewhere
else, like he was all along
in that moment with his brother
and didn't belong here.
Longing for a home still as boys,
he lives there now, having
walked from the barn at last,
broken and renewed.

ACKNOWLEDGMENTS

Poems from this volume have been published in the following journals:

The Write Launch "Harvest"
Dunes Review "Inheritance"
In Parentheses "Barn"
The Bryant Literary Review "Old Man," "Concrete," "At the Stockyard"
Tomahawk Creek Review "Enigma,"
Flying Island Literary Journal "Through the Peephole," "Ducklings," "Nisus and Euryalus"
Common Ground Review "Glass"
Delmarva Review "Dad's Naps"
Midway Journal "Logging"
The William and Mary Review "Ajax"
The Worcester Review: "Shoes"
The Emerson Review: "Broody," "Horses"
Pasque Petals: "Quilts"
Aletheia Literary Quarterly "Grade School Mythology," "The Boy and the Map"
West Trade Review: "Gun"
Aethlon: "Achilles"
Cathexis Northwest Press: "Beating," "Charity," "Words Like Ours"
East by Northeast: "Quotidian," "Skipping Stones"
Rappahannock Review: "Martha and Tooter"
Tar River Poetry: "Posts," "Pockets"
The Windhover: "Feet," "Presence"

"Raising the Hunley" was recorded for, and broadcast during, a segment of SCETV's *By the River*, a reading series with South Carolina poets.

My deepest gratitude to all of my friends, mentors, and teachers, who served diligently as readers and fellow revisers of these poems, most especially Tom Sleigh, Donna Masini, Catherine Barnett, William Wenthe, and Jan Cheripko—*Iron sharpeneth iron, so a man sharpeneth the countenance of his friend.*

Joshua Kulseth earned his BA in English from Clemson University, his MFA in poetry from Hunter College, and his PhD in poetry from Texas Tech University. He has co-authored two works of criticism and non-fiction—*Agony: Brazilian Jiu Jitsu and the Greeks,* and *W.H. Auden at Work: The Craft of Revision.* He is currently Assistant Professor of English and Creative Writing at Franciscan University of Steubenville.

www.ingramcontent.com/pod-product-compliance
Lightning Source LLC
Chambersburg PA
CBHW030057170426
43197CB00010B/1564